Dear Parents and Educators,

Welcome to Penguin Young Readers! As parents and educators, you know that each child develops at their own pace—in terms of speech, critical thinking, and, of course, reading. Penguin Young Readers recognizes this fact. As a result, each Penguin Young Readers book is assigned a traditional easy-to-read level (1–4) as well as an F&P Text Level (A–P). Both of these systems will help you choose the right book for your child. Please refer to the back of each book for specific leveling information. Penguin Young Readers features esteemed authors and illustrators, stories about favorite characters, fascinating nonfiction, and more!

Xavier Riddle and the Secret Museum: I am Mary Shelley	LEVEL **3**
	F&P TEXT LEVEL **M**

This book is perfect for a **Transitional Reader** who:
- can read multisyllable and compound words;
- can read words with prefixes and suffixes;
- is able to identify story elements (beginning, middle, end, plot, setting, characters, problem, solution); and
- can understand different points of view.

Here are some **activities** you can do during and after reading this book:
- Research: Mary Shelley was a famous writer of science fiction. Go to the library or use the internet to learn about science fiction and other famous science-fiction writers.
- Creative Writing: Xavier likes to tell silly stories; Mary likes to tell spooky stories. Write your own campfire story. Is it spooky, or silly, or something else?

Remember, sharing the love of reading with a child is the best gift you can give!

*This book has been officially leveled by using the F&P Text Level Gradient™ leveling system.

PENGUIN YOUNG READERS
An Imprint of Penguin Random House LLC, New York

Penguin supports copyright. Copyright fuels creativity, encourages diverse voices, promotes free speech, and creates a vibrant culture. Thank you for buying an authorized edition of this book and for complying with copyright laws by not reproducing, scanning, or distributing any part of it in any form without permission. You are supporting writers and allowing Penguin to continue to publish books for every reader.

© and TM 9 Story Media Group Inc. All rights reserved.

Published in 2021 by Penguin Young Readers, an imprint of Penguin Random House LLC, New York. Manufactured in China.

Visit us online at www.penguinrandomhouse.com.

ISBN 9780593225806 (pbk)   10 9 8 7 6 5 4 3 2 1
ISBN 9780593382608 (hc)   10 9 8 7 6 5 4 3 2 1

I am Mary Shelley

adapted by Marilyn Easton

Xavier is excited.

His Nature Troop is spending the night at the Secret Museum.

They will tell stories around a
campfire.

Xavier likes telling funny stories.

"Campfire stories should be
spooky. Not silly," says Yadina.

Xavier has never told a spooky story before.

He needs help.

"To the Secret Museum!" he says.

They wonder *who* they'll meet, and *where* they'll go, and *when*!

The friends see a feather.

It belonged to Mary Shelley.

She lived in England in 1805.

The friends place their hands on Berby.

"Ready for adventure?" Xavier asks.

They are transported back in time.

They see Mary Shelley writing a story with a feather.

"Pens and crayons did not exist
in 1805," Xavier whispers.

Mary is excited. It is her favorite part of the day. It is time for imagining!

Mary takes them to a field.

"Look at the clouds. Tell me what you see," says Mary.

Yadina sees a ghost.

Xavier sees a flying pumpkin pie. Then he sees a singing pizza. Then a line of ballerina fish!

But that is not spooky. That is silly.
Xavier can't help it. Silly ideas pop
into his head.

"That's the best part of imagining," says Mary. "You can tell stories your own way."

Mary looks at the clouds. She sees a castle. It is home to a wind monster.

Mary likes telling stories. She tells a spooky story about the wind monster.

"A story can be anything *you* want it to be," says Mary.

Xavier does not want to tell a
spooky story.

He likes to make people laugh.

"Silly stories are great!" Mary says.

"That's *your* way of telling a story."

"My way is with castles and
monsters and lightning bolts in
the sky," says Mary.

"Let your imagination run wild," Mary suggests. "Tell a story that's spooky and silly."

"Thanks, Mary!" Xavier calls.

It is time for the friends to leave.

Xavier tells his friends a campfire story. It is about a ghost.

The ghost is hunting for toes.

It wants to tickle them!

His friends laugh. It is a great story.